Published by Christian Focus Publications Ltd
Geanies House, Fearn, Tain, Ross-shire IV20 1TW www.christianfocus.com

Copyright © John Brown Brian Wright
ISBN: 978-1-5271-0946-9

This edition published in 2023
Cover illustration and internal illustrations by Lisa Flanagan
Cover and internal design by Lisa Flanagan
Printed and bound in China

All rights reserved. No part of this publication may be reproduced, stored in a retrieval system, or transmitted, in any form, by any means, electronic, mechanical, photocopying, recording or otherwise without the prior permission of the publisher or a licence permitting restricted copying. In the U.K. such licences are issued by the Copyright Licensing Agency, 4 Battlebridge Lane, London, SE1 2HX. www.cla.co.uk

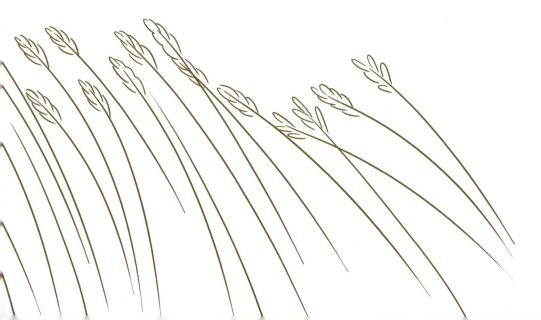

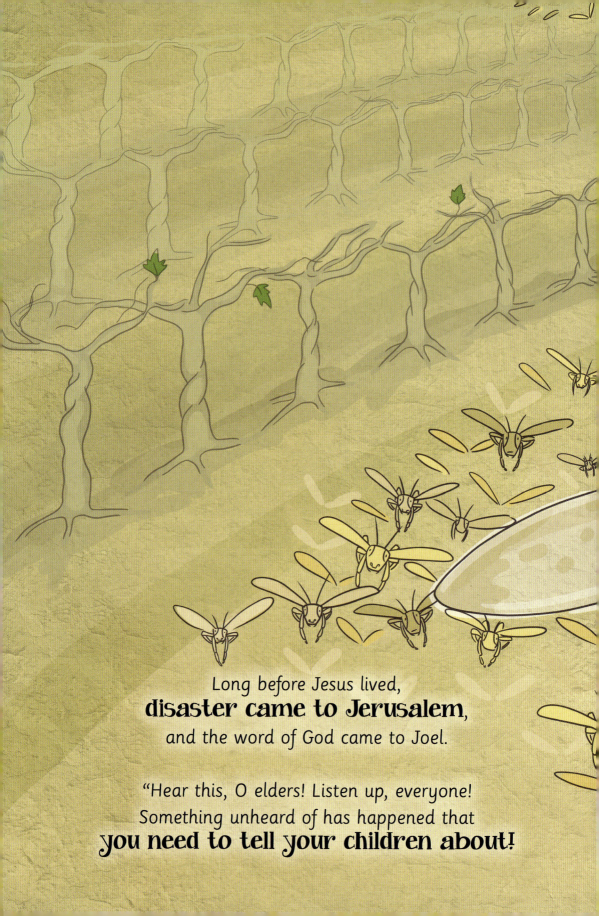

Long before Jesus lived,
disaster came to Jerusalem,
and the word of God came to Joel.

"Hear this, O elders! Listen up, everyone!
Something unheard of has happened that
you need to tell your children about!

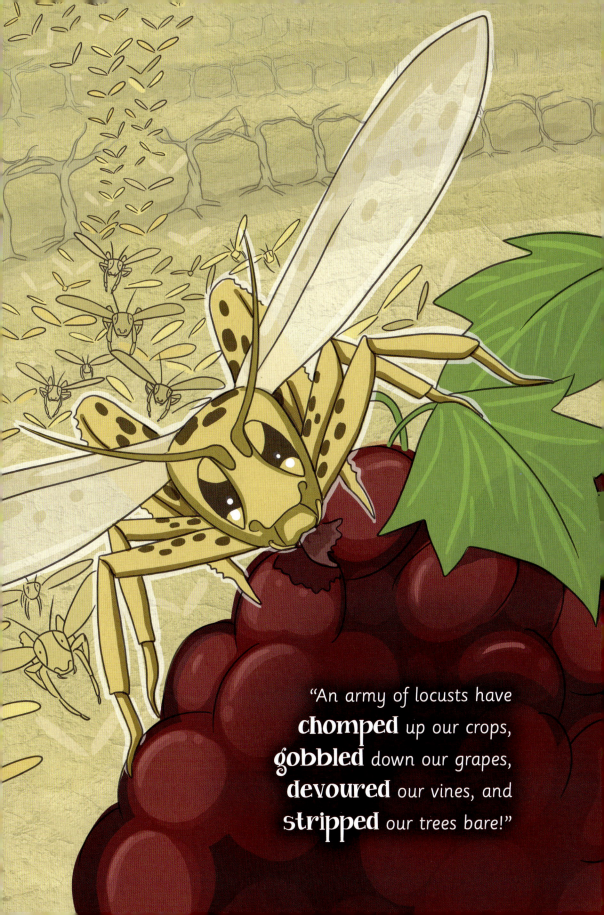

"An army of locusts have **chomped** up our crops, **gobbled** down our grapes, **devoured** our vines, and **stripped** our trees bare!"

"Not only this, but a **drought** has dried up our fields, our groves, our streams, our joy."

God had warned Israel long ago that He would send these disasters if they refused to obey Him.

"Weep, newlyweds!

Mourn, priests!

Despair, farmers!

Grieve, grape growers! Wail, everyone!
For **everything is ruined!"**

"Put on sackcloth, you priests! Pray all night for forgiveness! Announce a fast! Assemble everyone at the temple to **cry out to God for mercy!**

"**The day of the Lord is near**, when God Almighty will destroy those who disobey Him!"

"Our **food** is gone, our **fields** are burnt, our **streams** are dry, our **cattle** wander, and our **sheep** suffer.

"I cry out to you, O Lord, and even the animals groan in longing for you! **Have mercy on us! Save us!**"

God heard Joel and told him of a day in the future, **"the day of the Lord,"** when He will come with His angelic army to set things right.

But setting things right means judging wicked people, so **everyone must repent** and call on God right now while there is still time!

"Yet even now," says the Lord, "I will forgive you if you repent and return to Me with all your heart. Don't just pretend to be sorry; **prove it!**"

The Lord is gracious and compassionate, slow to anger and abounding in lovingkindness. He **forgives** those who truly repent.

"**Stop** everything!
Blow a trumpet!
Announce a fast!

Gather everyone, from the elders to nursing infants — even the bride and groom about to be married!"

Let the priests weep and say, "**Have compassion** on Your people, O Lord."

"Then **the Lord will forgive** His people and restore the rain and the grain, the grapes and the olive oil — everything the locusts ate and the drought dried up."

"God will drive out His people's enemies, and the land will be **free from fear** and **full of joy**, for the Lord has done great things."

You will have **plenty to eat** and **always be satisfied**, and you will praise the name of the Lord your God who has treated you so wonderfully.

You will know by these blessings that **I am with you**, and that **I am the Lord your God**; and that there is no other god; and that My people will never be put to shame.

"In those days,
I will pour out My Holy Spirit
on all My people — not just on judges like Samson and kings like David — but on everyone — male and female, old and young, slave and free."

"You will know when this happens because some will **prophesy**, some will dream **dreams**, and some will see **visions**."

"I will announce the day of the Lord with **signs for all to see**. The sun will turn dark, the moon will look blood-red, and there will be blood and fire and columns of smoke."

"In that day, **whoever calls upon the name of the Lord will be saved,** for He will spare those whom He chooses."

"But **the Lord is a refuge** for His people. 'Then you will know that I am the Lord your God who dwells in Jerusalem, making it **holy and safe forever**.'"

"In that day the mountains will **drip with wine**, the hills will **flow with milk**, the brooks will **gush with water**, and a spring from the Lord's house will water the Valley of Shittim.

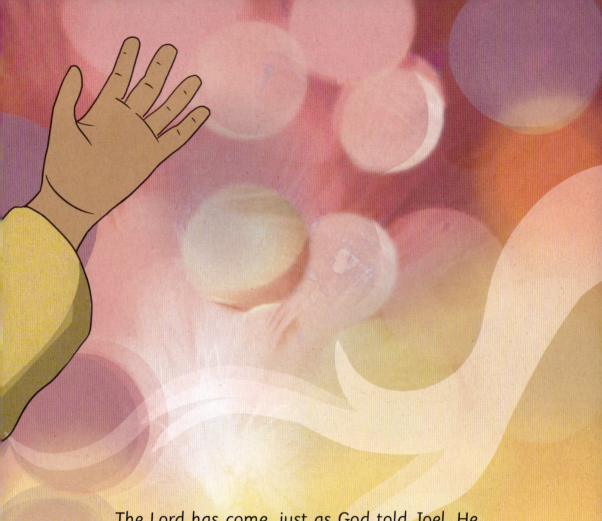

The Lord has come, just as God told Joel. He came as Jesus, and **whoever calls on the name of the Lord Jesus will be saved** and will receive the Holy Spirit just as God promised through Joel!

And **the Lord Jesus is coming back some day!** When He does, He will judge the wicked but forgive those who have repented and trusted in Him. Then He will restore the earth and live with His people forever and forever!

Christian Focus Publications publishes books for adults and children under its four main imprints: Christian Focus, CF4K, Mentor, and Christian Heritage. Our books reflect our conviction that God's Word is reliable and that Jesus is the way to know Him, and live for ever with Him.

Our children's publication list covers pre-school to early teens. We also publish personal and family devotionals, biographies and inspirational stories that children will love.

From pre-school board books to teenage apologetics, we have it covered!

Christian Focus Publications Ltd,
Geanies House, Fearn, Ross-shire,
IV20 1TW, Scotland,
United Kingdom.
www.christianfocus.com

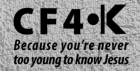

CF4•K
Because you're never
too young to know Jesus

Published by Christian Focus Publications Ltd
Geanies House, Fearn, Tain, Ross-shire IV20 1TW www.christianfocus.com

Copyright © John Brown Brian Wright
ISBN: 978-1-5271-0945-2

This edition published in 2023
Cover illustration and internal illustrations by Lisa Flanagan
Cover and internal design by Lisa Flanagan
Printed and bound in China

All rights reserved. No part of this publication may be reproduced, stored in a retrieval system, or transmitted, in any form, by any means, electronic, mechanical, photocopying, recording or otherwise without the prior permission of the publisher or a licence permitting restricted copying. In the U.K. such licences are issued by the Copyright Licensing Agency, 4 Battlebridge Lane, London, SE1 2HX. www.cla.co.uk

John Brown
Brian Wright

And it happened long ago that
a man named Jonah
lived near Nazareth,
where Jesus grew up.

One day God told Jonah,
"Get up! **Go to Nineveh**,
the great city, and warn them that
I know how bad they've been."

So Jonah got up and went ...
but not to Nineveh!
Instead, he went in the opposite direction. God said to go northeast to Nineveh, but Jonah boarded a ship sailing southwest to Tarshish.

So **God sent a great storm**
that was tearing the ship apart!

The sailors tried to row back to shore, but **the storm was too strong**.

So they prayed, "O Lord, please don't punish us because of him!"

Then they picked Jonah up and threw him into the sea. As soon as they did, **the storm stopped!** And they offered a sacrifice and made vows to Jonah's God.

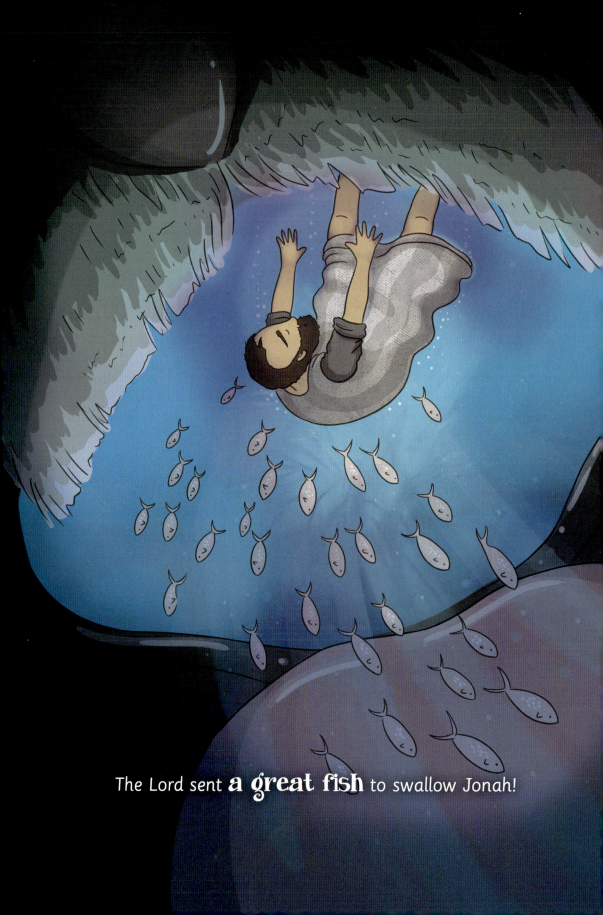

And Jonah spent **three days and nights** in the fish's stomach.

Then, when Jonah could sink no lower, he prayed:

"When I was in trouble, I cried out to God, and He answered me! **I called to you from the deep,** and You heard me!"

"You threw me into the deep and buried me beneath your waves. But even though you cast me from You, still **I will look to you for rescue!**"

"Water covered me; seaweed wrapped around my head. **I sank down** to the bottom of the sea and was trapped."

"But you brought me back,
O Lord my God,
even from this deep pit!
While I was slipping away,
I remembered the Lord,
and you heard my prayer!"

"Those who worship false gods
miss out on the mercy they could have had.
But as for me,
I will offer a sacrifice of thanksgiving,
for salvation belongs to the Lord!"

As soon as Jonah finished praying, the Lord commanded the fish to spit Jonah out onto dry land.

God again told Jonah, "Get up! Go to Nineveh, the great city, and say to them what I tell you." And **this time Jonah obeyed** and went.

Jonah went into the massive city of Nineveh and shouted out God's message:

The people of **Nineveh believed God and repented**. They stopped eating food and put on black, scratchy clothing to show they were sad for being so bad.

Even the king repented! He took off his robe and put on a black, scratchy shirt and sat in ashes. Then he issued an order for the entire city:

"Let no one eat a bite or drink a drop, not even animals!

Everyone must wear scratchy clothes, even our animals.

Everyone stop doing bad things and hurting people and ask God to spare us!"

"Who knows? When God sees how sorry we are for being bad, **maybe He will stop being angry** at us and decide not to destroy us."

When God saw the Ninevites repent, **He was merciful** and did not destroy them.

Jonah was angry, however, and left the city to see what would happen. "I knew you would show mercy, Lord! That's why I ran away! I'd rather die than live!"

The Lord **God sent a plant** to shade Jonah from the sun. Jonah was happy about the plant.

The next day, though, **God sent a worm** to eat the plant. Then **God sent a scorching wind**, and as the sun beat down Jonah grew faint and said, "I'd rather die than live!"

Then God said to Jonah, "**Are you right to be angry** that the plant died?"

You care about this plant, which you didn't cause to grow and which lived and died in a day.

Should I not care about Nineveh, which has more than 120,000 people who do not know right from wrong, plus all the animals?"

God taught Jonah some **important lessons**, which we need to learn as well. We should **care for all people**, because God cares for all people — even those who do bad things, like the Ninevites.

We should **never run away from God!**
We should obey Him instantly, completely, and cheerfully,
no matter what He tells us to do.

We should **pray to God** no matter what we've done or
what situation we're in. The Lord is sovereign over storms and
seas, fish and plants, winds and worms — over everything!
And He is gracious to forgive us when we repent of our sins.

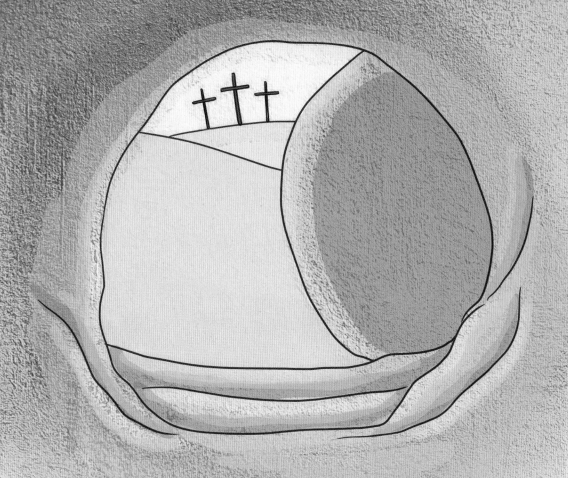

This is why God sent His Son Jesus, who died on the cross for our sins and then rose from the dead. And do you know what Jesus called His resurrection?
"The sign of Jonah".

Just as Jonah spent three days in the great fish, so Jesus spent three days in the grave.

But Jonah only seemed to come back from the dead, whereas Jesus actually died and rose again! Jesus was indeed **"something greater than Jonah"!**

So when you think of Jonah, think of Jesus. And remember that God who loved the Ninevites so much that He sent Jonah to warn them, loves you so much that
He sent Jesus to save you.

Jonah was right —
Salvation is from the Lord!

Christian Focus Publications publishes books for adults and children under its four main imprints: Christian Focus, CF4K, Mentor, and Christian Heritage. Our books reflect our conviction that God's Word is reliable and that Jesus is the way to know Him, and live for ever with Him.

Our children's publication list covers pre-school to early teens. We also publish personal and family devotionals, biographies and inspirational stories that children will love.

From pre-school board books to teenage apologetics, we have it covered!

Christian Focus Publications Ltd,
Geanies House, Fearn, Ross-shire,
IV20 1TW, Scotland,
United Kingdom.
www.christianfocus.com

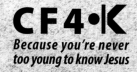

Published by Christian Focus Publications Ltd
Geanies House, Fearn, Tain, Ross-shire IV20 1TW www.christianfocus.com

Copyright © John Brown Brian Wright
ISBN: 978-1-5271-0947-6

This edition published in 2023
Cover illustration and internal illustrations by Lisa Flanagan
Cover and internal design by Lisa Flanagan
Printed and bound in China

All rights reserved. No part of this publication may be reproduced, stored in a retrieval system, or transmitted, in any form, by any means, electronic, mechanical, photocopying, recording or otherwise without the prior permission of the publisher or a licence permitting restricted copying. In the U.K. such licences are issued by the Copyright Licensing Agency, 4 Battlebridge Lane, London, SE1 2HX. www.cla.co.uk

Nahum
& the ninevites

John Brown
Brian Wright

"Good news!
Peace! *Shalom!*"

"**Celebrate** your sacred feasts! Fulfill your vows to God! For the evil Assyrians will never invade you again, for God is going to completely destroy them!"

The Assyrians were cruel warriors who conquered northern Israel and threatened the south.

And though their capital city **Nineveh** had repented when Jonah came, they later returned to their wicked ways.

So God gave a message concerning Nineveh, **the book of the vision of Nahum**.

"The Lord is jealous for His people and takes **vengeance on His enemies**. Though He is slow to anger, He will most certainly not leave the guilty unpunished but reserves wrath for His foes."

"God is good, a strong refuge in times of trouble;
He cares for those who trust in Him.

To Israel God says, "Though the Assyrians are mighty and many,
I will destroy them. I have finished punishing you, and now
I will break off their yoke and tear off your shackles."

The Lord will renew the land that enemies ruined and **restore Israel** to its former splendor.

But to Nineveh God says, "Whatever plots you are devising against God, He will destroy! **He will consume His enemies**, who are entangled in thorns, stumbling like drunks, and will be burnt like stubble!"

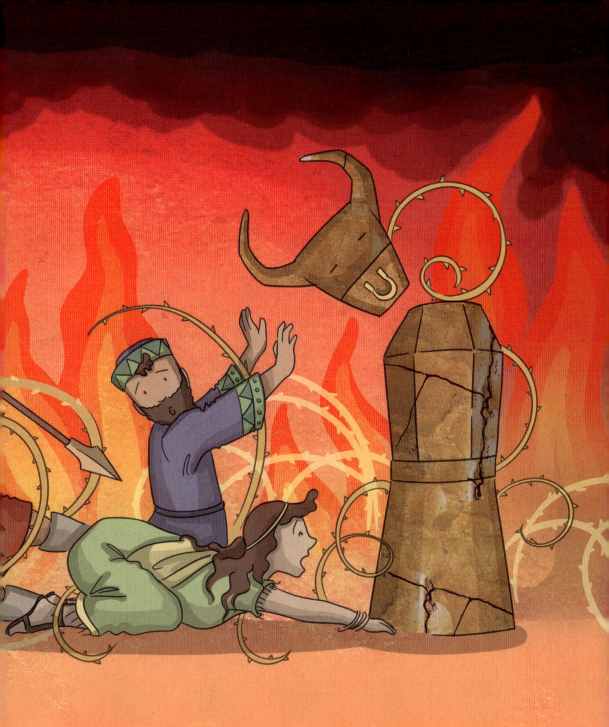

"I will end your dynasty, tear down your idols, and prepare your grave, **for you are despicable!**

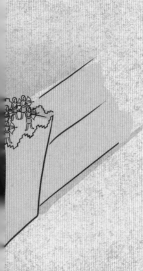

"An invader!
Guard the fort!
Watch the roads!
Summon the troops!
Get ready for battle!"

The invaders' **spears slash!**
Their **horses dash!**
Their **chariots flash!**
Their best soldiers stumble in
their rush to scale the walls!

"Maidens moan and beat their breasts. **Hearts** are melting, **knees** are knocking, **bodies** are shaking, and **faces** pale!"

"Where now is Nineveh,
that **den of proud lions**
who prowled fearlessly, fed freely,
and filled their lair with prey?"

"Behold, **I am against you!**" declares the Lord of hosts. "I will burn your chariots, strike down your cubs, end your hunting, and silence your messengers!"

Cracking whips! Rumbling chariots! Galloping horsemen! Flashing swords! Gleaming spears! **Dead bodies everywhere!**

And why will this happen?
Because Nineveh enticed and
enslaved many nations **like a
seductive sorceress.**

Therefore **I will humiliate her
publicly**, and none will feel sad for
her destruction or comfort her.

"Egypt's capital, Thebes, was a secure city with a river barrier, strong walls, and mighty allies — just like you, Nineveh. Yet **you defeated it** and took its people captive."

"And now **you will be defeated**, Nineveh, and forced to flee. Your fortresses will fall like figs. Your warriors are weak and your gates stand wide open with their bars burning."

"Go ahead and fortify your forts and store up supplies for the siege. **You will still be struck down** by the sword and consumed by fire."

"Multiply your soldiers like locusts and your officers like stars. Though they gather together tightly, **your leaders will all fly away** like locusts when the fighting starts!"

Your shepherds are sleeping, **your nobles** are lying down, and **your people** are scattered like sheep on the mountains with no one to regather them.

Your wound is fatal and **your destruction** is final, and all who hear of **your downfall** will clap their hands with joy, for who have you not wronged?

Nahum's name means "comfort," but there was nothing comforting in his book for God's enemies!

Those who hurt other people and worship other gods and refuse to repent will most certainly face God's terrible judgment, for **He does not leave the guilty unpunished.**

However, for God's people Nahum's prophecy is comforting indeed, for it assures us that **God will defeat all our enemies** so that we can worship and serve Him without fear.

This is why God sent His Son Jesus — **to defeat sin, death, and the devil** and to save all who repent of their sins and embrace Him as Savior and Lord.

And once we receive
the good news of the gospel,
we share it with others.

As the apostle Paul wrote to the Romans, quoting Nahum: "**Everyone who calls on the name of the Lord will be saved**. But how can they call on Him to save them unless they believe in Him? And how can they believe in Him if they have never heard about him? ... That is why the Scriptures say, "How beautiful are the feet of messengers who bring good news!"

Christian Focus Publications publishes books for adults and children under its four main imprints: Christian Focus, CF4K, Mentor, and Christian Heritage. Our books reflect our conviction that God's Word is reliable and that Jesus is the way to know Him, and live for ever with Him.

Our children's publication list covers pre-school to early teens. We also publish personal and family devotionals, biographies and inspirational stories that children will love.

From pre-school board books to teenage apologetics, we have it covered!

Christian Focus Publications Ltd,
Geanies House, Fearn, Ross-shire,
IV20 1TW, Scotland,
United Kingdom.
www.christianfocus.com

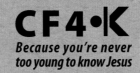

Published by Christian Focus Publications Ltd
Geanies House, Fearn, Tain, Ross-shire IV20 1TW www.christianfocus.com

Copyright © John Brown Brian Wright
ISBN: 978-1-5271-0944-5

This edition published in 2023
Cover illustration and internal illustrations by Lisa Flanagan
Cover and internal design by Lisa Flanagan
Printed and Bound in China

All rights reserved. No part of this publication may be reproduced, stored in a retrieval system, or transmitted, in any form, by any means, electronic, mechanical, photocopying, recording or otherwise without the prior permission of the publisher or a licence permitting restricted copying. In the U.K. such licences are issued by the Copyright Licensing Agency, 4 Battlebridge Lane, London, SE1 2HX. www.cla.co.uk

John Brown
Brian Wright

God had been so good to Israel!

He brought them back from Babylon, rebuilt the temple under Zerubbabel, restored worship under Ezra, and repaired Jerusalem's walls under Nehemiah!

But Israel was disobeying God, **again**.
So God withheld His blessings, **again**.
He also sent them His messenger Malachi
to tell them to repent and do right.

"**I've loved you!**," says the Lord.
But you say, "How have you loved us?"

"I've loved you by choosing Jacob over His brother Esau. I've blessed Jacob's descendants, the Israelites, but judged Esau's descendants, the Edomites -- who have been your constant enemies."

"Even if Edom rebuilds their cities,
I will knock down Edom's cities no matter
how many times they rebuild them!"

"Their country will be called 'The Land of Wickedness'.
Their people will be nicknamed, "Those who Always
Anger God".

"You will see me do this to Edom and say,
"The Lord is great even outside of Israel!"

"I will glorify my name among all the nations, from the rising of the sun in the east to its setting in the west. People everywhere will pray to Me and honor Me with pure offerings! You are dishonoring Me, but I will make My name great everywhere!"

"I wish someone would shut the temple doors so the priests couldn't offer their worthless sacrifices!," says the Lord. **I am not pleased with you**, so I won't accept your offerings!"

"I warn you, priests, if you do not repent and honor Me, then **I will punish you!**," says the Lord.

"Priests should teach truth and promote obedience, but you turned your backs on Me and cause others to do the same. Therefore I have exposed your wrongdoing, because **you are not obeying Me!**"

Having rebuked the priests, Malachi addressed the people again.

"Don't we all have the same Father? Weren't we all created by the same God? Then **why are we betraying and mistreating each other?**"

"Not only this, some are **betraying God** by marrying foreign women who worship false gods!

"The Lord of Heaven's Armies will cast out everyone who does this and reject their offerings!"

"You wonder why the Lord no longer accepts your offerings. I'll tell you why! You're **betraying your wives** whom you promised to take care of when you married them!"

"**I hate divorce**," says the Lord, the God of Israel. "So don't send your wives away just because you don't love them anymore and want to marry someone else! Don't be unfaithful!"

"But **who can endure the day when he comes** or stand before him when he arrives?

"He will be like a refining fire burning away impurities and like laundry soap washing away filth."

"**He will purify the priests** like silver and gold, so that they may present righteous offerings to the Lord. Then the Lord will be pleased with Israel's offerings like He was in olden days."

"Then **I will come to render swift judgement** against everyone who practices magic, betrays their wife, and breaks their vows.

I will judge those who take advantage of poor workers, widows, and orphans, who refuse to help foreigners, and who do not fear Me."

Yet if you will return to Me,
I will return to You.

But you say,
'How do we return to You?'"

"Will someone really steal from God? Yet **you are stealing from Me**" But you say, "How have we stolen from You?"

"You stole from Me when you refused to bring Me your tithes and offerings, which is why your nation is cursed."

"But if you bring me what you owe Me, then I will open heaven's floodgates and pour out blessings until they overflow. I will keep insects from eating your crops and make sure your vines grow grapes.

"Then all the nations will call you blessed, for **your land will be delightful**," says the Lord.

"You have spoken harsh words against Me," says the Lord. But you say, 'What have we said against you?'

"You said,
'It's useless serving God!
We could have done evil and gotten away with it.'"

But the Lord wrote down the names of those who fear Him in **a scroll of remembrance**.

"For behold, the day is coming when all the arrogant and everyone who does evil will be completely **burnt up like stubble** in a blazing furnace."

"But for you who revere My name, the sun of righteousness will rise with healing wings."

"You will skip like calves loosed from their stall and trample on the ashes of the wicked," says the Lord of hosts.

"Obey all the laws I gave to Moses for Israel on Mount Sinai."
"Behold, **I will send Elijah the prophet** before the great and dreadful day of the Lord.

"**He will turn the hearts** of fathers to their children and the hearts of children to their fathers lest I come and strike the land with a curse."

God did just like He said. **He sent John the Baptist** in the spirit and power of Elijah to turn the hearts of fathers back to their children and to prepare the way for the Lord.

John **preached for people to repent** of their arrogant evil-doing so that the Lord would forgive their sins.

John also told people that **Jesus was the Lamb of God** who takes away the sins of the world!

Jesus is the Sunrise from on high who came as the light of the world to lead us out of the dark shadow of death and into the path of peace!

The Lord Jesus did come into His temple! And Jesus is returning to judge the wicked and heal those who revere God and have faith in His Son!

Malachi's final message was also God's last words in the Hebrew Scriptures, as God sent Malachi to prepare His people for His Messiah, who is Jesus Christ the Lord.

Christian Focus Publications publishes books for adults and children under its four main imprints: Christian Focus, CF4K, Mentor, and Christian Heritage. Our books reflect our conviction that God's Word is reliable and that Jesus is the way to know Him, and live for ever with Him.

Our children's publication list covers pre-school to early teens. We also publish personal and family devotionals, biographies and inspirational stories that children will love.

From pre-school board books to teenage apologetics, we have it covered!

Christian Focus Publications Ltd,
Geanies House, Fearn, Ross-shire,
IV20 1TW, Scotland,
United Kingdom.
www.christianfocus.com

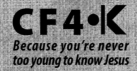